KINGDOM KEYS

These Key Bible Studies Belong to:

Date Started

Date Completed

His Ancient Ways
Publishing

Copyright © 2023 by Nancy B. Kline
All rights reserved.
Published by His Ancient Ways Publishing
ISBN 979-8-9879411-1-9

Contact: info@hisancientways.com
Website: www.hisancientways.com

CONTENTS

Free Resources

Free Gift

hisancientways.com/kk-gift

You Tube

youtube.com/@hisancientways

BIBLE READING TRACKER

Gen	1	2	3	4	5	6	7	8	9	10	11	12	13	14	15	16	17	18	19	20
21	22	23	24	25	26	27	28	29	30	31	32	33	34	35	36	37	38	39	40	41
42	43	44	45	46	47	48	49	50	Exo	1	2	3	4	5	6	7	8	9	10	11
12	13	14	15	16	17	18	19	20	21	22	23	24	25	26	27	28	29	30	31	32
33	34	35	36	37	38	39	40	Lev	1	2	3	4	5	6	7	8	9	10	11	12
13	14	15	16	17	18	19	20	21	22	23	24	25	26	27	Num	1	2	3	4	5
6	7	8	9	10	11	12	13	14	15	16	17	18	19	20	21	22	23	24	25	26
27	28	29	30	31	32	33	34	35	36	Deu	1	2	3	4	5	6	7	8	9	10
11	12	13	14	15	16	17	18	19	20	21	22	23	24	25	26	27	28	29	30	31
32	33	34	Josh	1	2	3	4	5	6	7	8	9	10	11	12	13	14	15	16	17
18	19	20	21	22	23	24	Judg	1	2	3	4	5	6	7	8	9	10	11	12	13
14	15	16	17	18	19	20	21	Ruth	1	2	3	4	1Sam	1	2	3	4	5	6	7
8	9	10	11	12	13	14	15	16	17	18	19	20	21	22	23	24	25	26	27	28
29	30	31	2Sam	1	2	3	4	5	6	7	8	9	10	11	12	13	14	15	16	17
18	19	20	21	22	23	24	1Kgs	1	2	3	4	5	6	7	8	9	10	11	12	13
14	15	16	17	18	19	20	21	22	2Kgs	1	2	3	4	5	6	7	8	9	10	11
12	13	14	15	16	17	18	19	20	21	22	23	24	25	1Chr	1	2	3	4	5	6
7	8	9	10	11	12	13	14	15	16	17	18	19	20	21	22	23	24	25	26	27
28	29	2Chr	1	2	3	4	5	6	7	8	9	10	11	12	13	14	15	16	17	18
19	20	21	22	23	24	25	26	27	28	29	30	31	32	33	34	35	36	Ezra	1	2
3	4	5	6	7	8	9	10	Neh	1	2	3	4	5	6	7	8	9	10	11	12
13	Esth	1	2	3	4	5	6	7	8	9	10	Job	1	2	3	4	5	6	7	8
9	10	11	12	13	14	15	16	17	18	19	20	21	22	23	24	25	26	27	28	29
30	31	32	33	34	35	36	37	38	39	40	41	42	Psa	1	2	3	4	5	6	7
8	9	10	11	12	13	14	15	16	17	18	19	20	21	22	23	24	25	26	27	28
29	30	31	32	33	34	35	36	37	38	39	40	41	42	43	44	45	46	47	48	49
50	51	52	53	54	55	56	57	58	59	60	61	62	63	64	65	66	67	68	69	70
71	72	73	74	75	76	77	78	79	80	81	82	83	84	85	86	87	88	89	90	91
92	93	94	95	96	97	98	99	100	101	102	103	104	105	106	107	108	109	110	111	112
113	114	115	116	117	118	119	120	121	122	123	124	125	126	127	128	129	130	131	132	133
134	135	136	137	138	139	140	141	142	143	144	145	146	147	148	149	150	Prov	1	2	3
4	5	6	7	8	9	10	11	12	13	14	15	16	17	18	19	20	21	22	23	24
25	26	27	28	29	30	31	Eccl	1	2	3	4	5	6	7	8	9	10	11	12	
Song	1	2	3	4	5	6	7	8	Isa	1	2	3	4	5	6	7	8	9	10	11
12	13	14	15	16	17	18	19	20	21	22	23	24	25	26	27	28	29	30	31	32
33	34	35	36	37	38	39	40	41	42	43	44	45	46	47	48	49	50	51	52	53
54	55	56	57	58	59	60	61	62	63	64	65	66	Jer	1	2	3	4	5	6	7
8	9	10	11	12	13	14	15	16	17	18	19	20	21	22	23	24	25	26	27	28
29	30	31	32	33	34	35	36	37	38	39	40	41	42	43	44	45	46	47	48	49
50	51	52	Lam	1	2	3	4	5	Ezek	1	2	3	4	5	6	7	8	9	10	11
12	13	14	15	16	17	18	19	20	21	22	23	24	25	26	27	28	29	30	31	32
33	34	35	36	37	38	39	40	41	42	43	44	45	46	47	48	Dan	1	2	3	4
5	6	7	8	9	10	11	12	Hos	1	2	3	4	5	6	7	8	9	10	11	12
13	14	Joel	1	2	3	Amos	1	2	3	4	5	6	7	8	9	Obad	1	Jon	1	2
3	4	Mic	1	2	3	4	5	6	7	Nah	1	2	3	Hab	1	2	3	Zeph	1	2
3	Hag	1	2	Zech	1	2	3	4	5	6	7	8	9	10	11	12	13	14	Mal	1
2	3	4	Matt	1	2	3	4	5	6	7	8	9	10	11	12	13	14	15	16	17
18	19	20	21	22	23	24	25	26	27	28	Mark	1	2	3	4	5	6	7	8	9
10	11	12	13	14	15	16	Luke	1	2	3	4	5	6	7	8	9	10	11	12	13
14	15	16	17	18	19	20	21	22	23	24	John	1	2	3	4	5	6	7	8	9
10	11	12	13	14	15	16	17	18	19	20	21	Acts	1	2	3	4	5	6	7	8
9	10	11	12	13	14	15	16	17	18	19	20	21	22	23	24	25	26	27	28	
Rom	1	2	3	4	5	6	7	8	9	10	11	12	13	14	15	16	1Cor	1	2	3
4	5	6	7	8	9	10	11	12	13	14	15	16	2Cor	1	2	3	4	5	6	7
8	9	10	11	12	13	Gal	1	2	3	4	5	6	Eph	1	2	3	4	5	6	
Phil	1	2	3	4	Col	1	2	3	4	1The	1	2	3	4	5	2The	1	2	3	
1Tim	1	2	3	4	5	6	2Tim	1	2	3	4	Tit	1	2	3	Phlm	1	Heb	1	2
3	4	5	6	7	8	9	10	11	12	13	Jas	1	2	3	4	5	1Pet	1	2	3
4	5	2Pet	1	2	3	1Joh	1	2	3	4	5	2Joh	1	3Joh	1	Jude	1	Rev	1	2
3	4	5	6	7	8	9	10	11	12	13	14	15	16	17	18	19	20	21	22	

INDEX & THEME TRACKER

Date	Page #	Passage	Themes	Entry #

INDEX & THEME TRACKER

Date	Page #	Passage	Themes	Entry #

INDEX & THEME TRACKER

Date	Page #	Passage	Themes	Entry #

Introduction to
Kingdom Keys Self-Guided Bible Study

Welcome to Kingdom Keys. I'm so glad this journal has found it's way into your hands and I've been praying it would be a blessing to you as you dig into God's Word. Let me share why I made this journal.

I've been a Christian for 20 years but I didn't engage deeply during my Bible reading time. Over time the Holy Spirit started convicting me of my lack of engagement in God's Word. So when it was time for me to buy a new Bible 4 years ago I decided I needed to get a study Bible to help me become engaged with what I was reading.

It worked. To the point where I needed to start taking notes. So I started Bible journaling in a notebook. To be clear, my style of Bible journaling is all about note-taking and not about artwork (I'm not against that but I'm not artistic). As I started taking notes, I played around with quite a few different systems and styles. I eventually landed on a system that became this journal.

This journal-style isn't the only component of my "system." I engage with my Bible many different ways. But this is the the system I use most often when I feel the need to study and meditate on a specific *passage* of scripture.

In the next section there's an instructional guide on the different elements in the journal but first I want to go over who this journal is for and how it might fit into your time with God.

Kingdom Keys is a mixture of different study and engagement disciplines. It's an Inductive Study method (observing context and applying Scripture). But it's also part Scripture Writing, and part Verse Mapping (deep dive study method). It takes the SOAP method (**S**cripture, **O**bserve, **A**pply, **P**ray) up a level but doesn't go quite as far as a full-blown Verse Mapping session might take you.

It's designed to make you seek understanding, yet the outcome (for me anyway) often results in profound revelation that goes beyond just "learning" as I'm seeking to understand. It will take you at least 45 minutes to an hour to complete, but it could be less than that if you're working with a single verse.

This journal has 90 entry spreads with simple "key" prompts to remind you of the purpose of each section. What you read, meditate and study is up to you. That's why this is called a "self-guided Bible study." It's for you to engage deeper with Scripture when the Holy Spirit prompts you. You can use it daily or just as you feel led to dig a little deeper with the time you have to dedicate to study.

There's flexibility built within this journal to move through the sections as you're led by the Holy Spirit, which is why I don't ask "prompting questions." There's also flexibility built into the layout so that you aren't "confined" to premade boxes in the sections that require more attention.

I've made this journal a little bigger than usual because this type of study needs room to breath. Yet even with this bigger size I sometimes go over my allotted space. When this happens I just finish my thoughts on a 4x6 post-it note and stick it right on the page. You could also do a "tip-in/out" which is a method of adding in your own page. When I have a lot of space left I will sometimes leave it or I will decorate with stickers. If you're artistic you can use that space for Holy Spirit inspired artwork.

The Biblical Concept of "Keys to the Kingdom"

Before getting into each section, lets explore just a little bit about how the kingdom of God and keys are represented in Scripture. I encourage you to do your own deep-dive study on this if you so wish. But here's just a few verses to explore.

Keys represent access and authority:

> **18** I *am* He who lives, and was dead, and behold, I am alive forevermore. Amen. **And I have the keys of Hades and of Death.**
> *Revelation 1:18*

Jesus has been given authority over death and now he can grant that authority over death to us. But only if we accept Him as Lord and Savior:

> **16** Simon Peter answered and said, "You are the Christ, the Son of the living God." **17** Jesus answered and said to him, "Blessed are you, Simon Bar-Jonah, for flesh and blood has not revealed *this* to you, but My Father who is in heaven. **18** And I also say to you that you are Peter, and on this rock I will build My church, and the gates of Hades shall not prevail against it. **19 And I will give you the keys of the kingdom of heaven,** and whatever you bind on earth will be bound in heaven, and whatever you loose on earth will be loosed in heaven."
> *Matthew 16:19-18*

Peter recognized Jesus as the Christ, the son of God and Jesus promised him "keys" to the Kingdom. But how did Jesus say we (not just Peter) should approach the kingdom of heaven?

> **31** "Therefore do not worry, saying, 'What shall we eat?' or 'What shall we drink?' or 'What shall we wear?' **32** For after all these things the Gentiles seek. For your heavenly Father knows that you need all these things. **33 But seek first the kingdom of God and His righteousness,** and all these things shall be added to you. *Matthew 6:31-33*

So how do we seek the kingdom? The kingdom of heaven and the kingdom of God are somewhat interchangeable in Scripture. It refers to where God resides, but also to his ultimate reign on earth and over His people. So we aren't seeking a "place" as much as we are seeking The King. And how do we do that?

By seeking Him in The Bible, and through prayer. All of God's attributes are in the Old Testament and the New Testament. We need to seek Him *there.*

Instructions for Kingdom Keys Bible Study Journal

I will use Matthew 25:1-13 to illustrate how I would work through each section.
I encourage you to read that passage as you're going through these instructions.

Header: Included here are checkboxes to help you remember to do certain things as you're studying: pray, track your entry in the journal tracker, and annotate.

Pray: You should always pray that the Holy Spirit will reveal understanding to you before you read and study the Bible. This checkbox will ensure you don't foget.

Annotate: Something you can skip if you want. But this is what I do: when I am journaling a portion of scripture I want to mark it in my Bible so I know I've journaled about it. So I place a code in my Bible near the passage that tells me where it's at. Like this: SJ10 = "Study Journal Entry 10."

I don't use page numbers for this because I want to carry the number on through the next journal I'm using. This is my system but you can skip this if you want.

Track: Trackers are located at the beginning of the journal. It's a place for you to track the entirety of the scriptures you've read and also a place for you to track the individual passages. I've included a place to write the themes of each passage because you may find yourself drawn to passages about similar themes and it'll help you recognize that. You start with the page number of the journal so you can easily find your way to that entry when re-visiting this journal. But it also tells you the entry # in the journal so if you see that in a future reading of the Bible you can see exactly where to find that in this journal.

Entry #: This is the entry number of the journal if you would like to try out my system.

Passage: This is the complete passage you are reading that day.

Kingdom Key: CONTEXT. As we are seeking Him through His Word there is one thing we need to know:

> **16** All Scripture *is* given by inspiration of God, and *is* profitable for doctrine, for reproof, for correction, for instruction in righteousness. ~ *2 Timothy 3:16*

This means that the Bible can't contradict itself. So if we think it does, we are in error. And the best way to figure out why it *doesn't* is to understand and keep the context of the passage in mind.

The word "context" isn't in the Bible itself but the concept is. For instance, 1 & 2 Chronicals takes place roughly at the same time as 2 Samual and 1 & 2 Kings but is from the vantage point of a Priest. It was written after the 70 years of Babylonian captivity, yet it pertains to years before the capitivity. It was written to reconnect the Jewish exiles with their ancestry as much of it was lost during their captivity. Without knowing this you might get confused as to why there's another book of the bible describing David's Kingship. The people would have known exactly why this portion of Scripture was written.

Keeping context in mind is also of great importance when reading the Epistles because they were letters written to specific groups of people for specific reasons. Knowing the context is important for correct interpretation.

Understanding context is such an important aspect of Bible study that I consider it a "key" to understanding the Bible.

This is how you determine the context:

Who (who wrote it, to who, about who)
What (main point or themes)
Where (location)
When (when it was written or when something happened)
Why (reason for the writing or why something happened)
How (how something is done/accomplished, how someone is to respond)

I don't dedicate a lot of space and time on this as it will naturally come out more fully in other sections below. But the space given is enough to jot down a few main basics.

Matt 25:1-13 Example: *Matthew 25:1-13. Parable of the 10 virgins, Jesus teaching privately to his disciples on the Mount of Olives. They asked when and how He will come at the end of the age. He teaches on the importance of staying prepared for His coming.*

Themes: 1-3 single words or phrases that are take-away themes of the passage.

Kingdom Key: TRUTHS. Jesus said He is the way and the truth and the life (John 14:6). Paul said that all Scripture is Holy Spirit inspired and good for doctrine, correction and instruction (2 Timothy 3:16). So we have to know what truth is being revealed about what topic (themes). This may not be apparent to you right away, but it will flesh itself out as you dig deeper. You will put these in your tracker.

Matt 25:1-13 Example: *Preparedness, anointing, steadfastness & faithfullness.*

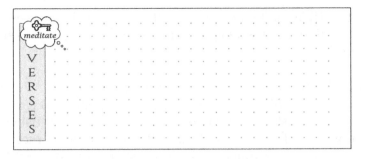

Verse: Write out the specific verse(s) you want to meditate upon. You can use the ellipses (...) to jump portions of scripture. This is not the entire passage but a shorter portion that you want to closely examine.

Kingdom Key: MEDITATE. Scripture writing is a meditation discipline that helps you slow down and focus on each and every word. It's an amazing way to meditate on the Word like God instructed in Joshua 1:8. Psalm 119 is an excellent portion of scripture that speaks of constantly meditating on God's word. Go slowly as you write out your verses and meditate on each word or phrase. You will dig into them in the next step.

Matt 25:1-13 Example: *I wrote out verses 2-5, 9 and 12.*

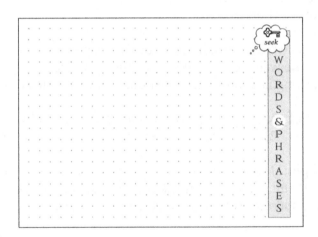

Words and Phrases: This is where you start examining the words and phrases in the verses you wrote down.

Kingdom Key: SEEK. There are a lot of verses about seeking God and His kingdom. Jesus said to seek first the kingdom of God (Matthew 6:33). He also said to ask, seek and knock (Matthew 7:7). God promises that if you seek Him you will find him if you seek with all your heart (Jeremiah 29:13). There are many more verses than this and I encourage you to seek them out.

An easy way to "seek" is to start doing word-studies. This is a component of Verse Mapping, where you look at the original language and defintions of words and phrases, looking at multiple translations and all cross references and then ultimately re-writing the verse you're studying.

However, Kingdom Keys is NOT a full-blown Verse Mapping system. So I keep my engagement here to finding repeated words and deciphering why they're being repeated, original language studies and the meaning of words and phrases.

How do I do this: I use a Bible app to access a Strong's Interlinear Bible for original word meanings; I use a regular dictionary; I will occasionally look up a commentary if I'm confused; I will sometimes look up a cross reference - especially if it's one that the Holy Spirit has brought to my mind.

I color code by circling, boxing, underlining, or highlighting words or phrases in the verses I wrote down, and then I use the same color to write out my findings in the SEEK section. The colors don't mean anything, I'm just using them to correlate where the word is in the verse I wrote out and what I wrote in the SEEK section.

Matt 25:1-13 Example: *I looked up the meanings of the following words: oil, flasks, enough, and know. I wrote down what I thought the following phrases meant: "not enough for us and for you," and "I do not know you." I wrote about the significance of who the "dealers" might be.*

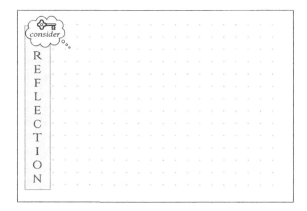

Reflection: This is where you begin deeply thinking about everything you just _seeked-out_ out in the WORDS & PHRASES section, also taking into account the _context_ you wrote down in the PASSAGE section. This is also where you will begin to recognize the _truths_ being conveyed for the THEMES section if you haven't already done so.

Kingdom Key: CONSIDER. The word "consider" is mentioned all throughout the Bible and can mean "understand," "discern" or "regard." Jesus used this word during the Sermon on the Mount in Matthew 6:28.

Starting in this section we begin to transition into an inductive study method. If you're familiar with the SOAP method then you know what inductive study is. (Again, SOAP stands for **S**cripture, **O**bserve, **A**pply, and **P**ray). The SOAP method is the most popular one there is but in my opinion most SOAP journals do not allow for deep engagement and lack instructional methods; although you certainly can use the SOAP method as a framework for deep engagement. However I love doing word studies so this is why I added in the previous Verse Mapping section.

In most inductive study methods there's an "observe" section or something like it. In Kingdom Keys the observe section begins by looking at the _context_ in the PASSAGE section, then _seeking_ in the WORDS & PHRASES section, and is finally expanded upon as we begin to _consider_ the passage in the REFLECTION section.

This is NOT the time for applying the passage just yet. Here you will begin to write out what you are seeing and hearing from the Holy Spirit. You may want to write out what you think is the most profound thing you're drawn to consider. There aren't any hard and fast rules here. You just sit with the Lord and write out what you're hearing. This portion of Kingdom Keys can become very revelatory for you if you're letting the Holy Spirit guide you. If you're struggling here then you can just attempt to re-write the main verse in your own words...that will get you thinking seriously about it.

Matt 25:1-13 Example: _I considered the following things: oil representing the Holy Spirit; who the wise followers are and what makes them wise; what makes the others foolish; what it meant that "all" were sleeping; why Jesus did not know them; why they didn't have their own oil; who they were getting their oil from._

Application: This is where you begin to think about how the passage can apply to yourself.

Kingdom Key: RENEW. There are many verses about being renewed by the Word of God but the main one is Romans 12:2 where Paul tells us we need to be transformed by the renewing of the mind. When we're born again our spirit is instantly renewed but our minds need time in the Word for renewal.

We have to allow the Word of God to renew our minds as we seek Him deeply in Scripture and prayer. That is why we need to apply Scripture to ourselves. I often find it easiest to ask myself a series of questions when attempting to apply scripture to myself (Have I done that? Am I doing that?)

Matt 25:1-13 Example: _I asked myself if I have been keeping the anointing of the Holy Spirit flowing in my life. I recognized that it's ok to get weary (since they were all sleeping but some were not left behind because of it). I recognized that I need to steadfastly and continually refill my lamp through reading, studying, praying and worshiping God every single day. I recognized that I cannot seek God just through doing churchy things and that I cannot receive my oil from anybody but the Holy Spirit. I recognized that I need to be on Jesus' radar at all times by asking, seeking and knocking._

Response: This is where you write out your response to God about what you just read. I really like the concept of "responding" to the Word of God.

Kingdom Key: PRAY. Jesus was always sneaking away to pray to the Father. We must do that as well.

Jesus tells us if we ask He will respond. This is what we're doing. We are responding by submitting our will to God and possibly petitioning Him if we feel ill-equipped to renew our minds as we wrote out in the APPLICATION section.

Matt 25:1-13 Example: *I repented for times when I got weary and lazy in my walk with Him. I thanked Him for His faithfulness towards me. I asked that the anointing of the Holy Spirit would be full and flowing in and through me. I asked for the strength to persevere while awaiting for Jesus to return.*

Final Comments

On the next next page is a quick-glance-guide for a quick and easy reminder if it's ever needed.

After that there are a few empty dot-grid pages for you to do with as you wish: extra trackers, artwork, notes, stickers, whatever.

One more note on how I set up this journal. It's fine if one section flows into the other. They aren't meant to be sections so much as "zones". For example, on the right hand spread , the upper zone is for Reflection, the middle zone is for Application and the bottom zone is for Response. When I'm done I usually take a highlighter and put a line differentiating between my "zones."

I pray this journal is a blessing to you as you apply these kingdom keys to unlock what God is showing you about His Kingdom.

~ Nancy B. Kline

QUICK GLANCE GUIDE

Section	Key	What	How
Passage	Context	What, Where, When, Who, Why, and How	Keep it brief. It will come out more in other sections.
Themes	Truths	The main truths being addressed.	1 to 3 single words or short phrases.
Verse(s)	Meditate	Write out a few verses to dig into.	Go slow. Meditate on each word. Uses (...) to jump verses.
Words & Phrases	Seek	Notice repeated words. Seek meanings of words. Note correlations or contrasts. Use an Interlinear Bible for word meanings. Use commentaries if necessary.	Circle, square, underline, highlight words/phrases in the verse you wrote then use the same color to write down your findings in the this section.
Reflection	Consider	Deeply reflect on everything you've learned so far.	Consider the themes, context and meanings. Listen to the Holy Spirit for revelation. Re-write the verses in your own words if you're struggling.
Application	Renew	Renew your mind by applying the passage to your life, or to your relationship with God.	Ask yourself questions based on your reflections.
Response	Pray	Respond to God's Word through Prayer.	Submit your will, repent, praise God and ask for help to apply what you wrote in the application section.

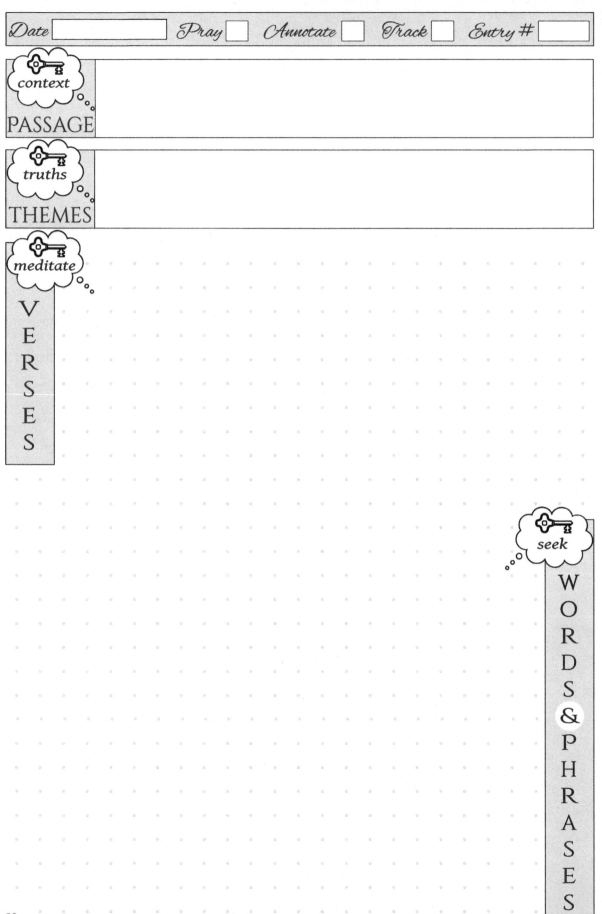

Date ☐ Pray ☐ Annotate ☐ Track ☐ Entry # ☐

context
PASSAGE

truths
THEMES

meditate
VERSES

seek
WORDS & PHRASES

20

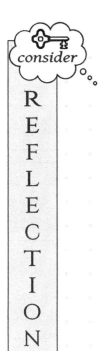

REFLECTION

consider

APPLICATION

renew

RESPONSE

pray

Date _____   Pray ☐   Annotate ☐   Track ☐   Entry # _____

context

PASSAGE

truths

THEMES

meditate

V
E
R
S
E
S

seek

W
O
R
D
S
&
P
H
R
A
S
E
S

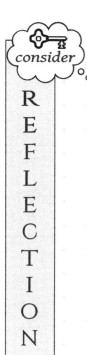

REFLECTION

consider

APPLICATION

renew

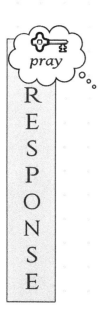

RESPONSE

pray

Date _____ Pray ☐ Annotate ☐ Track ☐ Entry # _____

context
PASSAGE

truths
THEMES

meditate
V E R S E S

seek
W O R D S & P H R A S E S

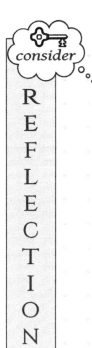

REFLECTION

consider

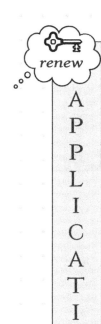

APPLICATION

renew

RESPONSE

pray

Date ⬚   Pray ⬚   Annotate ⬚   Track ⬚   Entry # ⬚

context
PASSAGE

truths
THEMES

meditate
VERSES

seek
WORDS & PHRASES

REFLECTION

consider

APPLICATION

renew

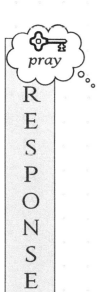

RESPONSE

pray

Date | Pray | Annotate | Track | Entry #

context

PASSAGE

truths

THEMES

meditate

VERSES

seek

WORDS & PHRASES

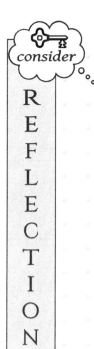

REFLECTION — *consider*

APPLICATION — *renew*

RESPONSE — *pray*

Date [   ] Pray [ ] Annotate [ ] Track [ ] Entry # [   ]

context
PASSAGE

truths
THEMES

meditate
V
E
R
S
E
S

seek
W
O
R
D
S
&
P
H
R
A
S
E
S

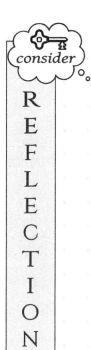

REFLECTION

APPLICATION

RESPONSE

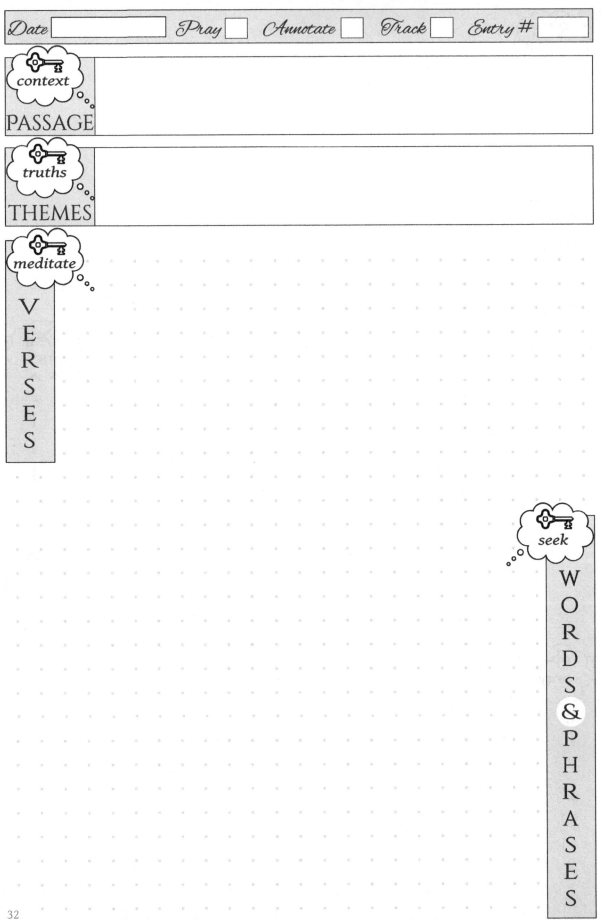

Date ____ Pray ☐ Annotate ☐ Track ☐ Entry # ____

context
PASSAGE

truths
THEMES

meditate
V E R S E S

seek
W O R D S & P H R A S E S

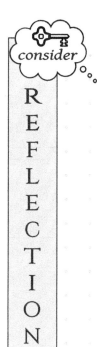

consider

REFLECTION

renew

APPLICATION

pray

RESPONSE

33

Date [   ]   Pray [ ]   Annotate [ ]   Track [ ]   Entry # [   ]

context
PASSAGE

truths
THEMES

meditate
V
E
R
S
E
S

seek
W
O
R
D
S
&
P
H
R
A
S
E
S

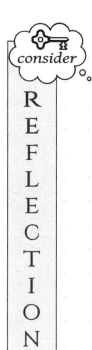

consider

REFLECTION

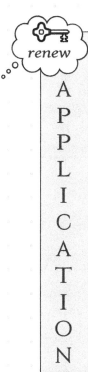

renew

APPLICATION

pray

RESPONSE

Date | Pray | Annotate | Track | Entry #

context

PASSAGE

truths

THEMES

meditate

VERSES

seek

WORDS & PHRASES

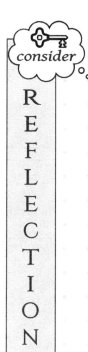

REFLECTION

consider

APPLICATION

renew

RESPONSE

pray

Date _____ Pray ☐ Annotate ☐ Track ☐ Entry # _____

context
PASSAGE

truths
THEMES

meditate
VERSES

seek
WORDS & PHRASES

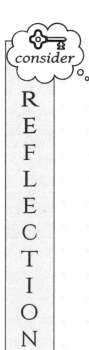

consider

REFLECTION

renew

APPLICATION

pray

RESPONSE

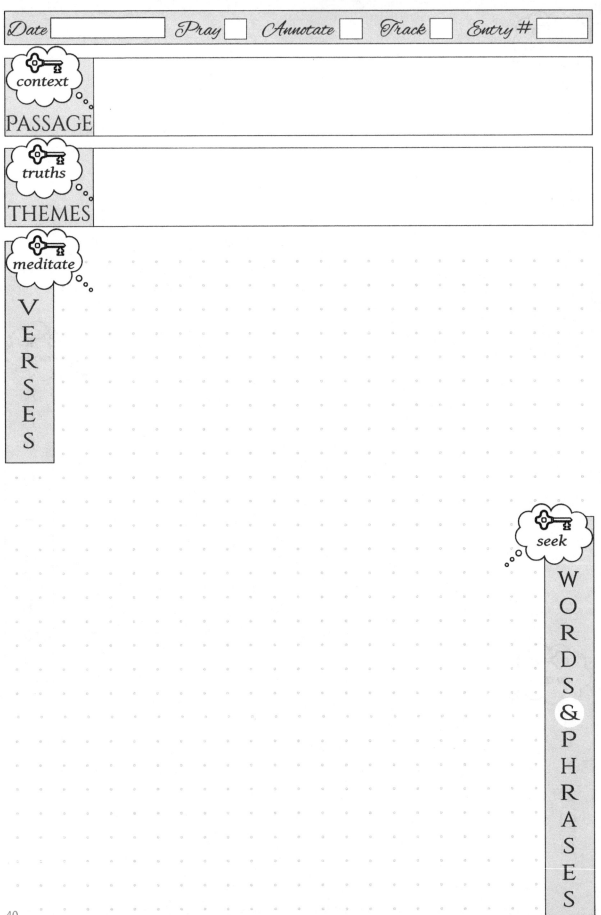

Date ☐ Pray ☐ Annotate ☐ Track ☐ Entry #

context
PASSAGE

truths
THEMES

meditate
VERSES

seek
WORDS & PHRASES

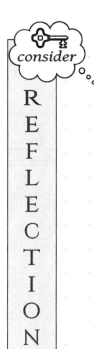

REFLECTION

consider

APPLICATION

renew

RESPONSE

pray

Date [   ] Pray [ ] Annotate [ ] Track [ ] Entry # [   ]

context
PASSAGE

truths
THEMES

meditate
V
E
R
S
E
S

seek
W
O
R
D
S
&
P
H
R
A
S
E
S

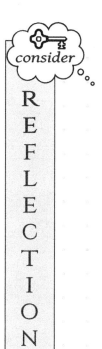

REFLECTION

RESPONSE

APPLICATION

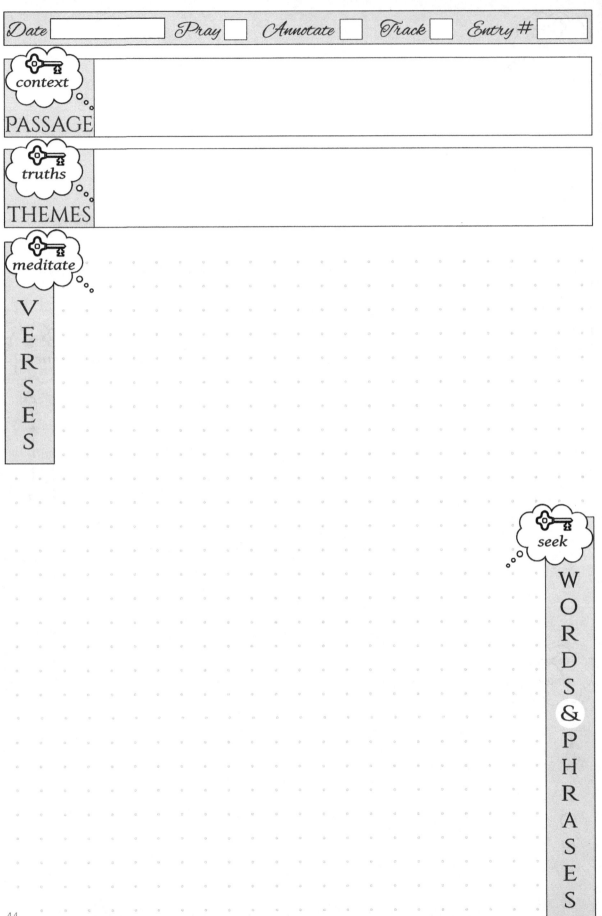

Date _____ Pray ☐ Annotate ☐ Track ☐ Entry # _____

context
PASSAGE

truths
THEMES

meditate
VERSES

seek
WORDS & PHRASES

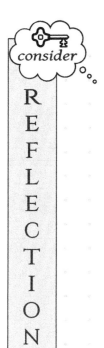

consider

REFLECTION

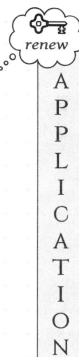

renew

APPLICATION

pray

RESPONSE

Date _____ Pray ☐ Annotate ☐ Track ☐ Entry # ___

context
PASSAGE

truths
THEMES

meditate
V
E
R
S
E
S

seek
W
O
R
D
S
&
P
H
R
A
S
E
S

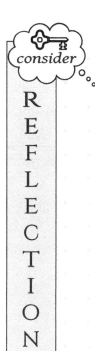

consider

REFLECTION

renew

APPLICATION

pray

RESPONSE

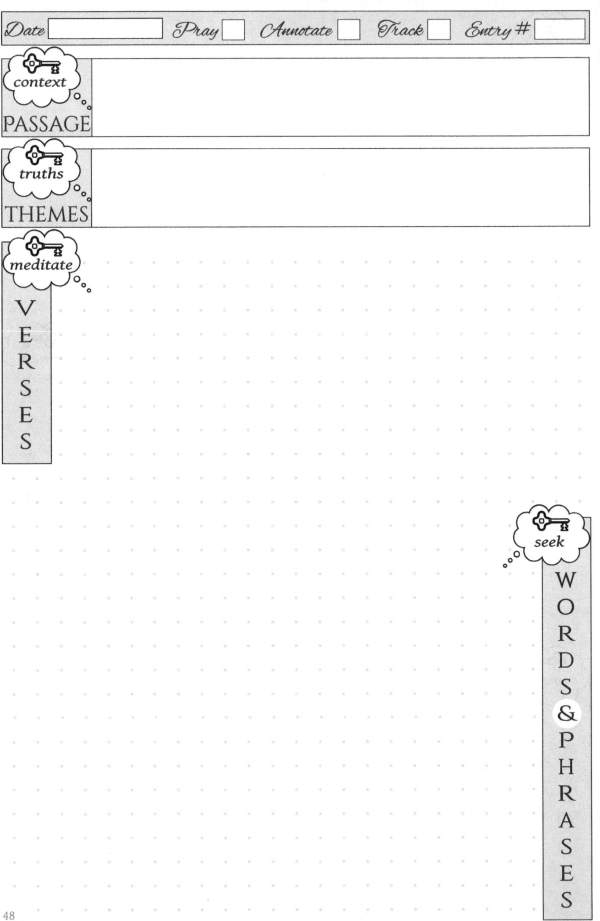

Date [ ] Pray [ ] Annotate [ ] Track [ ] Entry # [ ]

context
PASSAGE

truths
THEMES

meditate
VERSES

seek
WORDS & PHRASES

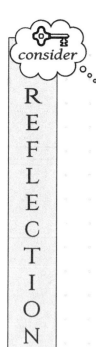

REFLECTION

consider

APPLICATION

renew

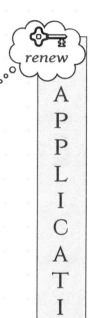

RESPONSE

pray

Date _____   Pray ☐   Annotate ☐   Track ☐   Entry # _____

context
PASSAGE

truths
THEMES

meditate
V
E
R
S
E
S

seek
W
O
R
D
S
&
P
H
R
A
S
E
S

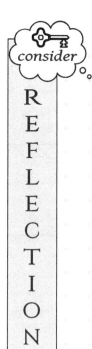

REFLECTION

consider

RESPONSE

pray

APPLICATION

renew

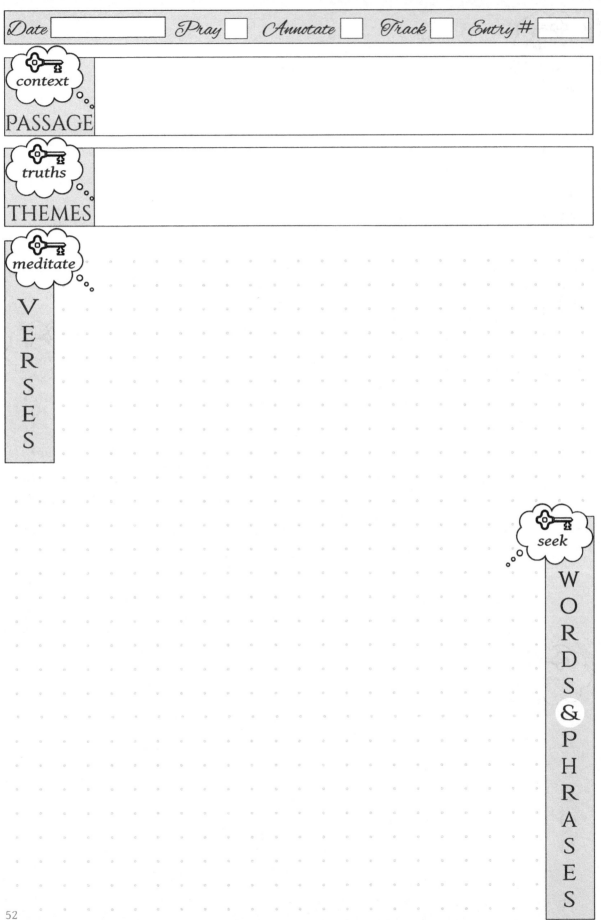

Date ____ Pray ☐ Annotate ☐ Track ☐ Entry # ____

context
PASSAGE

truths
THEMES

meditate
VERSES

seek
WORDS & PHRASES

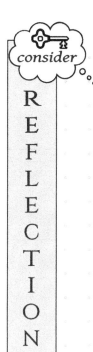

REFLECTION

consider

RESPONSE

pray

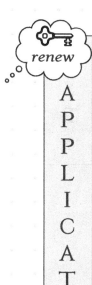

APPLICATION

renew

Date [   ] Pray [ ] Annotate [ ] Track [ ] Entry # [   ]

context
PASSAGE

truths
THEMES

meditate
V E R S E S

seek
WORDS & PHRASES

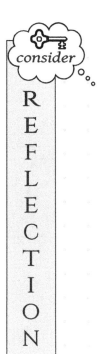

REFLECTION

consider

APPLICATION

renew
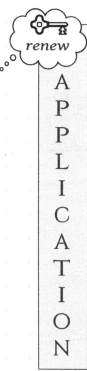

RESPONSE

pray

55

Date Pray Annotate Track Entry #

context

PASSAGE

truths

THEMES

meditate

VERSES

seek

WORDS & PHRASES

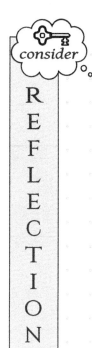

REFLECTION

consider

APPLICATION

renew

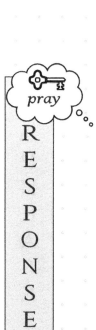

RESPONSE

pray

Date _____ Pray ☐ Annotate ☐ Track ☐ Entry # _____

context
PASSAGE

truths
THEMES

meditate
VERSES

seek
WORDS & PHRASES

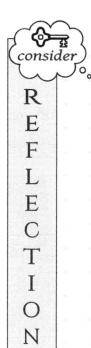

REFLECTION

consider

APPLICATION

renew

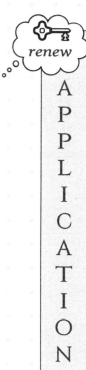

RESPONSE

pray

Date _____ Pray ☐ Annotate ☐ Track ☐ Entry # _____

context
PASSAGE

truths
THEMES

meditate
VERSES

seek
WORDS & PHRASES

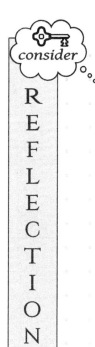

consider

REFLECTION

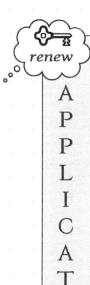

renew

APPLICATION

pray

RESPONSE

Date ☐ Pray ☐ Annotate ☐ Track ☐ Entry #

context

PASSAGE

truths

THEMES

meditate

VERSES

seek

WORDS & PHRASES

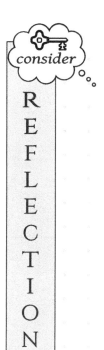

REFLECTION

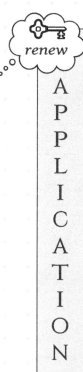

APPLICATION

RESPONSE

Date _____ Pray ☐ Annotate ☐ Track ☐ Entry # _____

context

PASSAGE

truths

THEMES

meditate

**V
E
R
S
E
S**

seek

**W
O
R
D
S
&
P
H
R
A
S
E
S**

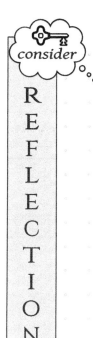

REFLECTION

APPLICATION

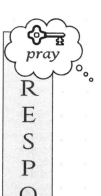

RESPONSE

Date _____ Pray ☐ Annotate ☐ Track ☐ Entry # ____

context
PASSAGE

truths
THEMES

meditate
V
E
R
S
E
S

seek
W
O
R
D
S
&
P
H
R
A
S
E
S

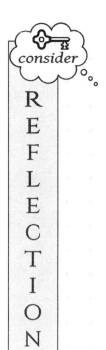

REFLECTION

consider

APPLICATION

renew

RESPONSE

pray

Date _____ Pray ☐ Annotate ☐ Track ☐ Entry # _____

context
PASSAGE

truths
THEMES

meditate
V E R S E S

seek
W O R D S & P H R A S E S

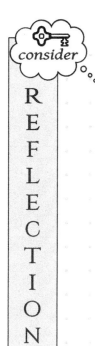

REFLECTION

consider

pray

RESPONSE

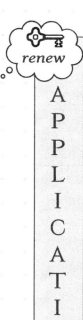

renew

APPLICATION

Date [   ] Pray [ ] Annotate [ ] Track [ ] Entry # [   ]

context

PASSAGE

truths

THEMES

meditate

V
E
R
S
E
S

seek

W
O
R
D
S
&
P
H
R
A
S
E
S

REFLECTION

consider

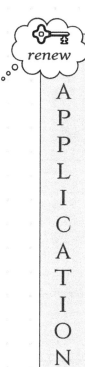

APPLICATION

renew

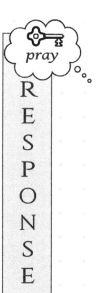

RESPONSE

pray

Date ☐ | Pray ☐ | Annotate ☐ | Track ☐ | Entry # ☐

context
PASSAGE

truths
THEMES

meditate
V E R S E S

seek
W O R D S & P H R A S E S

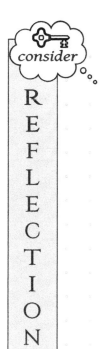

REFLECTION

consider

APPLICATION

renew

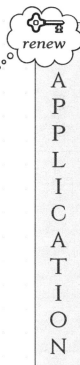

RESPONSE

pray

73

Date ☐ Pray ☐ Annotate ☐ Track ☐ Entry #

context
PASSAGE

truths
THEMES

meditate
V
E
R
S
E
S

seek
W
O
R
D
S
&
P
H
R
A
S
E
S

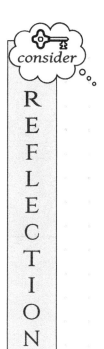

REFLECTION

consider

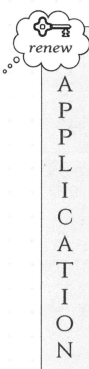

APPLICATION

renew

RESPONSE

pray

Date *Pray* *Annotate* *Track* *Entry #*

context

PASSAGE

truths

THEMES

meditate

VERSES

seek

WORDS & PHRASES

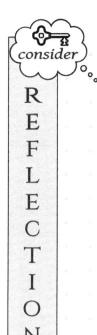

consider

REFLECTION

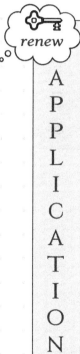

renew

APPLICATION

pray

RESPONSE

Date _____ Pray ☐ Annotate ☐ Track ☐ Entry # _____

context
PASSAGE

truths
THEMES

meditate
V
E
R
S
E
S

seek
W
O
R
D
S
&
P
H
R
A
S
E
S

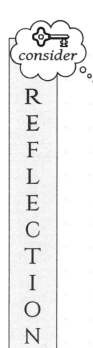

REFLECTION

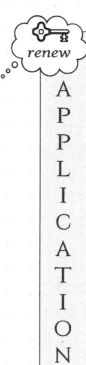

APPLICATION

RESPONSE

Date _____   Pray ☐   Annotate ☐   Track ☐   Entry # _____

context
PASSAGE

truths
THEMES

meditate
V
E
R
S
E
S

seek
W
O
R
D
S
&
P
H
R
A
S
E
S

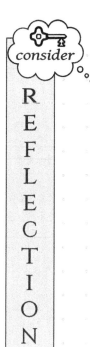

REFLECTION
consider

APPLICATION
renew

RESPONSE
pray

Date [ ]   Pray [ ]   Annotate [ ]   Track [ ]   Entry # [ ]

context

PASSAGE

truths

THEMES

meditate

VERSES

seek

WORDS & PHRASES

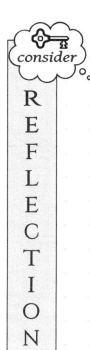

REFLECTION

consider

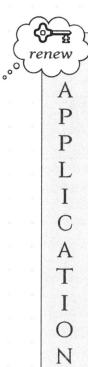

APPLICATION

renew

RESPONSE

pray

Date _____ Pray ☐ Annotate ☐ Track ☐ Entry # _____

context
PASSAGE

truths
THEMES

meditate
V
E
R
S
E
S

seek
W
O
R
D
S
&
P
H
R
A
S
E
S

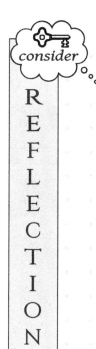

REFLECTION

consider

APPLICATION

renew

RESPONSE

pray

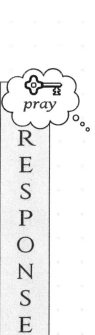

Date | Pray | Annotate | Track | Entry #

context

PASSAGE

truths

THEMES

meditate

VERSES

seek

WORDS & PHRASES

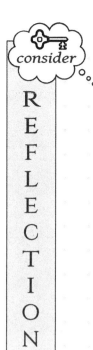

REFLECTION

consider

APPLICATION

renew

RESPONSE

pray

Date [   ] Pray [ ] Annotate [ ] Track [ ] Entry # [   ]

context
PASSAGE

truths
THEMES

meditate
VERSES

seek
WORDS & PHRASES

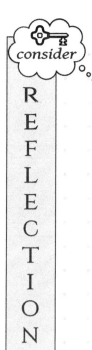

REFLECTION

consider

APPLICATION

renew

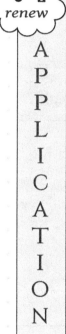

RESPONSE

pray

Date _____ Pray ☐ Annotate ☐ Track ☐ Entry # _____

context
PASSAGE

truths
THEMES

meditate
V
E
R
S
E
S

seek
W
O
R
D
S
&
P
H
R
A
S
E
S

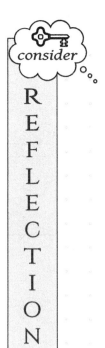

REFLECTION *consider*

RESPONSE *pray*

APPLICATION *renew*

Date _____ Pray ☐ Annotate ☐ Track ☐ Entry # _____

context
PASSAGE

truths
THEMES

meditate
V
E
R
S
E
S

seek
W
O
R
D
S
&
P
H
R
A
S
E
S

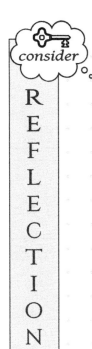

REFLECTION

consider

APPLICATION

renew
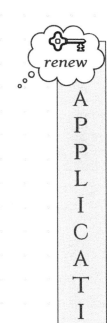

RESPONSE

pray

Date _____ Pray ☐ Annotate ☐ Track ☐ Entry # _____

context

PASSAGE

truths

THEMES

meditate

VERSES

seek

WORDS & PHRASES

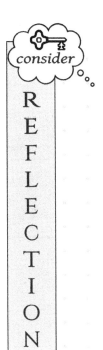

REFLECTION

consider

APPLICATION

renew

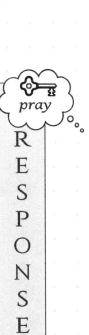

RESPONSE

pray

Date ☐ Pray ☐ Annotate ☐ Track ☐ Entry #

context

PASSAGE

truths

THEMES

meditate

V
E
R
S
E
S

seek

W
O
R
D
S
&
P
H
R
A
S
E
S

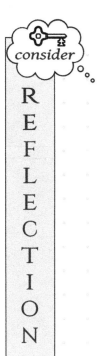

REFLECTION *consider*

APPLICATION *renew*

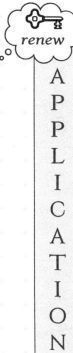

RESPONSE *pray*

Date [ ] Pray [ ] Annotate [ ] Track [ ] Entry # [ ]

context
PASSAGE

truths
THEMES

meditate
V
E
R
S
E
S

seek
W
O
R
D
S
&
P
H
R
A
S
E
S

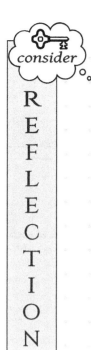

REFLECTION

consider

APPLICATION

renew

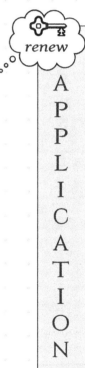

RESPONSE

pray

Date [   ]   Pray [ ]   Annotate [ ]   Track [ ]   Entry # [   ]

context
PASSAGE

truths
THEMES

meditate
VERSES

seek
WORDS & PHRASES

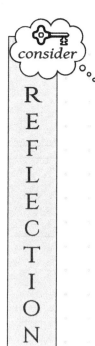

REFLECTION

consider

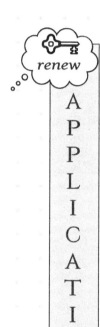

APPLICATION

renew

RESPONSE

pray

Date | Pray | Annotate | Track | Entry #

context

PASSAGE

truths

THEMES

meditate

VERSES

seek

WORDS & PHRASES

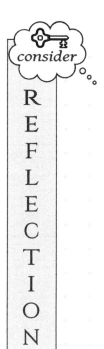

REFLECTION
consider

APPLICATION
renew
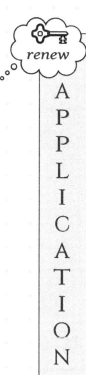

RESPONSE
pray

Date ☐ Pray ☐ Annotate ☐ Track ☐ Entry #

context

PASSAGE

truths

THEMES

meditate

V
E
R
S
E
S

seek

W
O
R
D
S
&
P
H
R
A
S
E
S

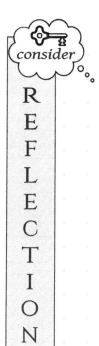

REFLECTION

consider

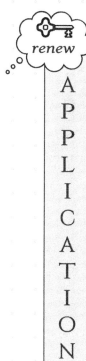

APPLICATION

renew

RESPONSE

pray

Date _____ Pray ☐ Annotate ☐ Track ☐ Entry # _____

context

PASSAGE

truths

THEMES

meditate

V
E
R
S
E
S

seek

W
O
R
D
S
&
P
H
R
A
S
E
S

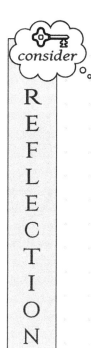

REFLECTION

consider

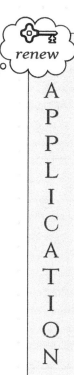

APPLICATION

renew

RESPONSE

pray

Date [   ] Pray [ ] Annotate [ ] Track [ ] Entry # [   ]

context
PASSAGE

truths
THEMES

meditate
VERSES

seek
WORDS & PHRASES

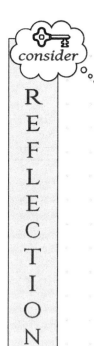

REFLECTION

consider

RESPONSE

pray

APPLICATION

renew

Date [   ]   Pray [ ]   Annotate [ ]   Track [ ]   Entry # [   ]

context

PASSAGE

truths

THEMES

meditate

V
E
R
S
E
S

seek

W
O
R
D
S
&
P
H
R
A
S
E
S

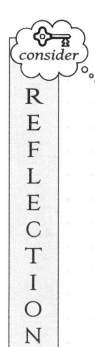

REFLECTION

consider

APPLICATION

renew

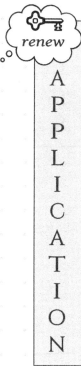

RESPONSE

pray

Date Pray Annotate Track Entry #

context

PASSAGE

truths

THEMES

meditate

VERSES

seek

WORDS & PHRASES

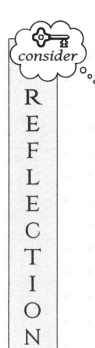

consider

REFLECTION

renew

APPLICATION

pray

RESPONSE

Date [　　　　] Pray [ ] Annotate [ ] Track [ ] Entry # [　　　　]

context

PASSAGE

truths

THEMES

meditate

V
E
R
S
E
S

seek

W
O
R
D
S
&
P
H
R
A
S
E
S

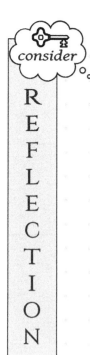

R
E
F
L
E
C
T
I
O
N

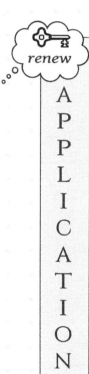

A
P
P
L
I
C
A
T
I
O
N

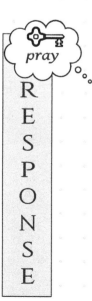

R
E
S
P
O
N
S
E

Date _____ Pray ☐ Annotate ☐ Track ☐ Entry # _____

context
PASSAGE

truths
THEMES

meditate
V
E
R
S
E
S

seek
W
O
R
D
S
&
P
H
R
A
S
E
S

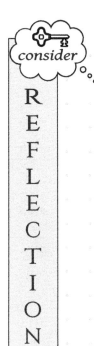

consider

REFLECTION

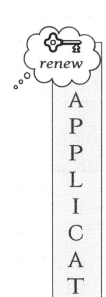

renew

APPLICATION

pray

RESPONSE

Date [   ] Pray [ ] Annotate [ ] Track [ ] Entry # [   ]

context
PASSAGE

truths
THEMES

meditate
V E R S E S

seek
W O R D S & P H R A S E S

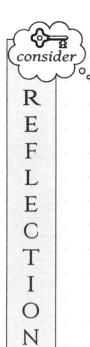

REFLECTION

RESPONSE

APPLICATION

Date _____ Pray ☐ Annotate ☐ Track ☐ Entry # _____

context
PASSAGE

truths
THEMES

meditate
V E R S E S

seek
W O R D S & P H R A S E S

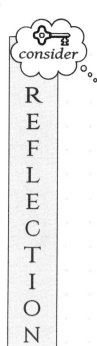

REFLECTION

consider

APPLICATION

renew

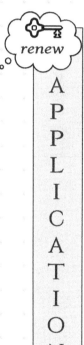

RESPONSE

pray

Date _____ Pray ☐ Annotate ☐ Track ☐ Entry # _____

context
PASSAGE

truths
THEMES

meditate
V
E
R
S
E
S

seek
W
O
R
D
S
&
P
H
R
A
S
E
S

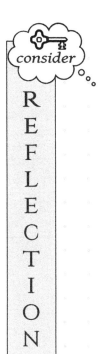

REFLECTION

consider

APPLICATION

renew

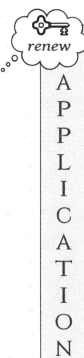

RESPONSE

pray

Date [   ] *Pray* ☐ *Annotate* ☐ *Track* ☐ Entry # [   ]

context
PASSAGE

truths
THEMES

meditate
V E R S E S

seek
W O R D S & P H R A S E S

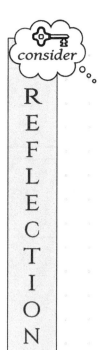

REFLECTION *consider*

APPLICATION *renew*

RESPONSE *pray*

Date ☐ Pray ☐ Annotate ☐ Track ☐ Entry # ☐

context
PASSAGE

truths
THEMES

meditate
V
E
R
S
E
S

seek
W
O
R
D
S
&
P
H
R
A
S
E
S

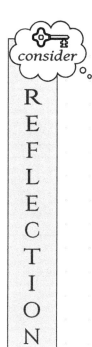

REFLECTION

consider

pray

RESPONSE

APPLICATION

renew

Date _____ Pray ☐ Annotate ☐ Track ☐ Entry # _____

context
PASSAGE

truths
THEMES

meditate
V
E
R
S
E
S

seek
W
O
R
D
S
&
P
H
R
A
S
E
S

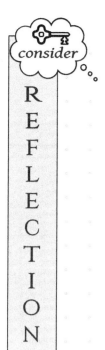

REFLECTION *consider*

APPLICATION *renew*

RESPONSE *pray*

Date _____ Pray ☐ Annotate ☐ Track ☐ Entry # _____

context
PASSAGE

truths
THEMES

meditate
V
E
R
S
E
S

seek
W
O
R
D
S
&
P
H
R
A
S
E
S

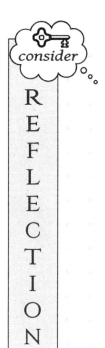

REFLECTION

consider

APPLICATION

renew

RESPONSE

pray

Date [   ]   Pray [ ]   Annotate [ ]   Track [ ]   Entry # [   ]

context
PASSAGE

truths
THEMES

meditate
V
E
R
S
E
S

seek
W
O
R
D
S
&
P
H
R
A
S
E
S

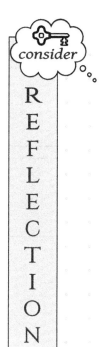

REFLECTION

consider

pray

RESPONSE

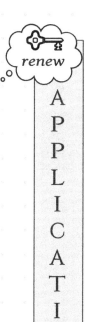

APPLICATION

renew

Date _____ Pray ☐ Annotate ☐ Track ☐ Entry # _____

context
PASSAGE

truths
THEMES

meditate
V
E
R
S
E
S

seek
W
O
R
D
S
&
P
H
R
A
S
E
S

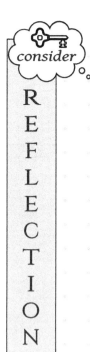

REFLECTION

consider

APPLICATION

renew

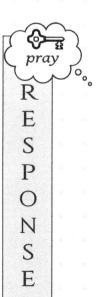

RESPONSE

pray

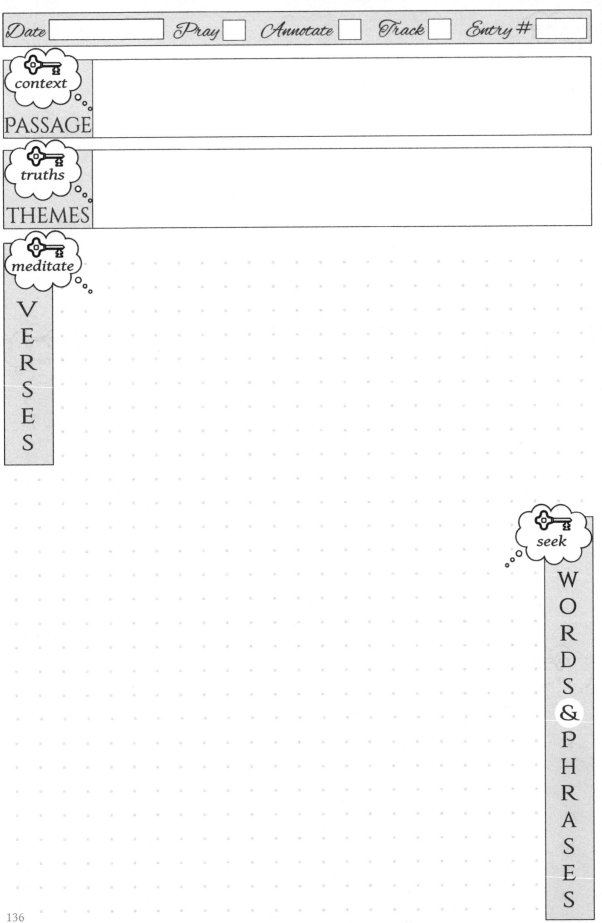

Date _____ Pray ☐ Annotate ☐ Track ☐ Entry # _____

context
PASSAGE

truths
THEMES

meditate
V E R S E S

seek
W O R D S & P H R A S E S

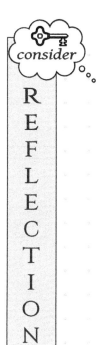

REFLECTION

consider

RESPONSE

pray

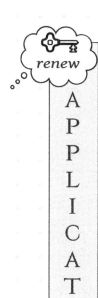

APPLICATION

renew

Date Pray Annotate Track Entry #

context

PASSAGE

truths

THEMES

meditate

VERSES

seek

WORDS & PHRASES

REFLECTION

consider

RESPONSE

pray

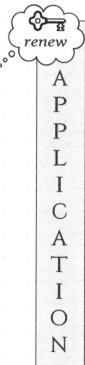

APPLICATION

renew

Date [   ] *Pray* [ ] *Annotate* [ ] *Track* [ ] *Entry #* [   ]

context
PASSAGE

truths
THEMES

meditate
V
E
R
S
E
S

seek
W
O
R
D
S
&
P
H
R
A
S
E
S

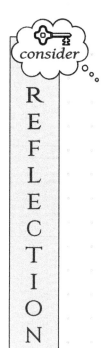

REFLECTION

consider

APPLICATION

renew

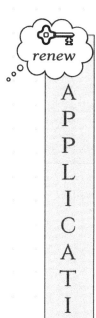

RESPONSE

pray

Date | Pray | Annotate | Track | Entry #

context

PASSAGE

truths

THEMES

meditate

VERSES

seek

WORDS & PHRASES

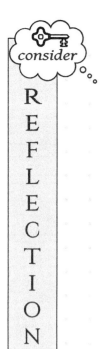

REFLECTION

consider

APPLICATION

renew

RESPONSE

pray

context

PASSAGE

truths

THEMES

meditate

VERSES

seek

WORDS & PHRASES

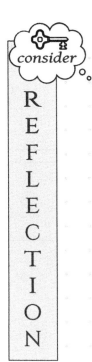

REFLECTION

consider

APPLICATION

renew

RESPONSE

pray

Date ☐ Pray ☐ Annotate ☐ Track ☐ Entry #

context
PASSAGE

truths
THEMES

meditate
V E R S E S

seek
W O R D S & P H R A S E S

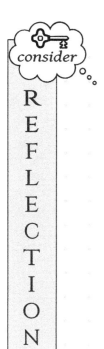

REFLECTION

consider

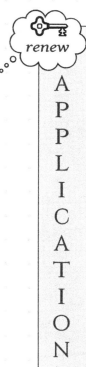

APPLICATION

renew

RESPONSE

pray

Date [　　　　　　] Pray ☐ Annotate ☐ Track ☐ Entry # [　　　　]

context
PASSAGE

truths
THEMES

meditate
VERSES

seek
WORDS & PHRASES

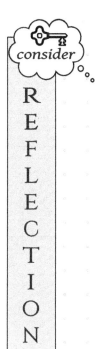

REFLECTION

consider

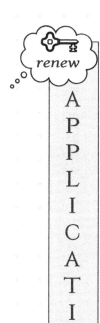

APPLICATION

renew

RESPONSE

pray

Date ☐ Pray ☐ Annotate ☐ Track ☐ Entry #

context
PASSAGE

truths
THEMES

meditate
V
E
R
S
E
S

seek
W
O
R
D
S
&
P
H
R
A
S
E
S

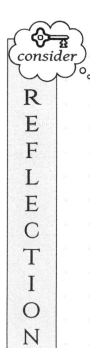

REFLECTION

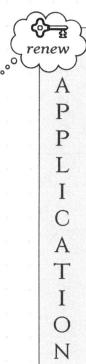

APPLICATION

RESPONSE

Date | Pray | Annotate | Track | Entry #

context
PASSAGE

truths
THEMES

meditate
VERSES

seek
WORDS & PHRASES

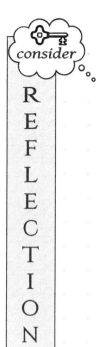

REFLECTION

consider

APPLICATION

renew

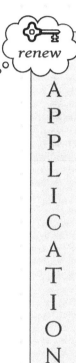

RESPONSE

pray

Date [   ] Pray [ ] Annotate [ ] Track [ ] Entry # [   ]

context
PASSAGE

truths
THEMES

meditate
V E R S E S

seek
W O R D S & P H R A S E S

REFLECTION

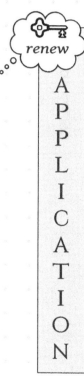

APPLICATION

RESPONSE

Date _____ Pray ☐ Annotate ☐ Track ☐ Entry # _____

context

PASSAGE

truths

THEMES

meditate

V
E
R
S
E
S

seek

W
O
R
D
S
&
P
H
R
A
S
E
S

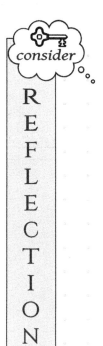

REFLECTION

consider

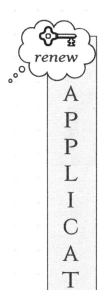

APPLICATION

renew

RESPONSE

pray

Date _____ Pray ☐ Annotate ☐ Track ☐ Entry # _____

context
PASSAGE

truths
THEMES

meditate
V
E
R
S
E
S

seek
W
O
R
D
S
&
P
H
R
A
S
E
S

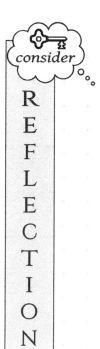

REFLECTION

APPLICATION

RESPONSE

Date [   ] Pray [ ] Annotate [ ] Track [ ] Entry # [   ]

context
PASSAGE

truths
THEMES

meditate
VERSES

seek
WORDS & PHRASES

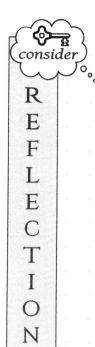

REFLECTION

consider

APPLICATION

renew

RESPONSE

pray

Date [ ] Pray [ ] Annotate [ ] Track [ ] Entry # [ ]

context
PASSAGE

truths
THEMES

meditate
V E R S E S

seek
W O R D S & P H R A S E S

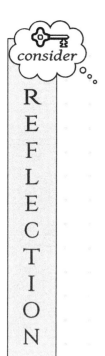

REFLECTION

consider

APPLICATION

renew

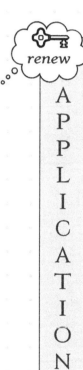

RESPONSE

pray

Date _____ Pray ☐ Annotate ☐ Track ☐ Entry # _____

context
PASSAGE

truths
THEMES

meditate
V
E
R
S
E
S

seek
W
O
R
D
S
&
P
H
R
A
S
E
S

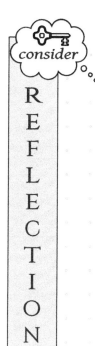

REFLECTION

consider

APPLICATION

renew

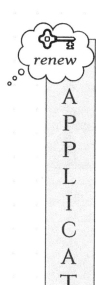

RESPONSE

pray

Date | Pray | Annotate | Track | Entry #

context
PASSAGE

truths
THEMES

meditate
VERSES

seek
WORDS & PHRASES

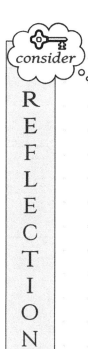

R
E
F
L
E
C
T
I
O
N

A
P
P
L
I
C
A
T
I
O
N

R
E
S
P
O
N
S
E

Date [ ] Pray [ ] Annotate [ ] Track [ ] Entry # [ ]

context
PASSAGE

truths
THEMES

meditate
VERSES

seek
WORDS & PHRASES

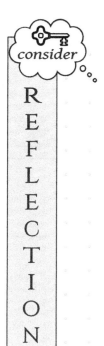

REFLECTION

consider

APPLICATION

renew

pray

RESPONSE

Date Pray Annotate Track Entry #

context

PASSAGE

truths

THEMES

meditate

VERSES

seek

WORDS & PHRASES

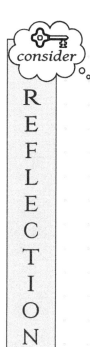

REFLECTION

consider

APPLICATION

renew

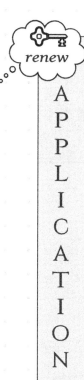

RESPONSE

pray

Date _____ Pray ☐ Annotate ☐ Track ☐ Entry # _____

context
PASSAGE

truths
THEMES

meditate
VERSES

seek
WORDS & PHRASES

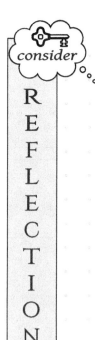

REFLECTION

consider

APPLICATION

renew

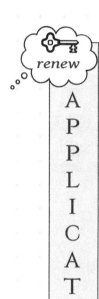

RESPONSE

pray

Date ☐   Pray ☐   Annotate ☐   Track ☐   Entry # ☐

context
PASSAGE

truths
THEMES

meditate
V E R S E S

seek
W O R D S & P H R A S E S

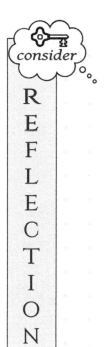

REFLECTION *consider*

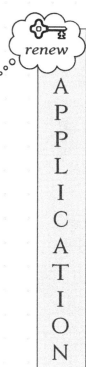

APPLICATION *renew*

RESPONSE *pray*

Date Pray Annotate Track Entry #

context

PASSAGE

truths

THEMES

meditate

VERSES

seek

WORDS & PHRASES

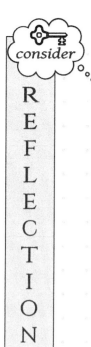

REFLECTION

consider

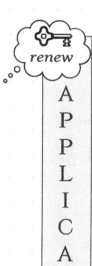

APPLICATION

renew

RESPONSE

pray

Date _____ Pray ☐ Annotate ☐ Track ☐ Entry # _____

context
PASSAGE

truths
THEMES

meditate
V
E
R
S
E
S

seek
W
O
R
D
S
&
P
H
R
A
S
E
S

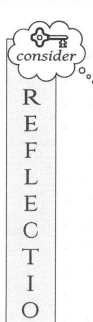

REFLECTION

consider

RESPONSE

pray

APPLICATION

renew

Date ☐ Pray ☐ Annotate ☐ Track ☐ Entry #

context

PASSAGE

truths

THEMES

meditate

V
E
R
S
E
S

seek

W
O
R
D
S
&
P
H
R
A
S
E
S

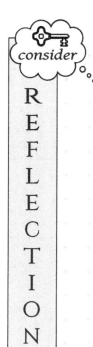

REFLECTION

consider

RESPONSE

pray

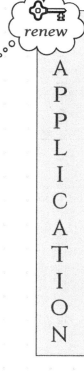

APPLICATION

renew

Date [   ] Pray [ ] Annotate [ ] Track [ ] Entry # [   ]

context
PASSAGE

truths
THEMES

meditate
V E R S E S

seek
W O R D S & P H R A S E S

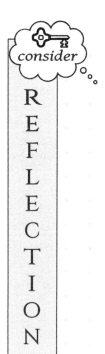

REFLECTION

consider

RESPONSE

pray

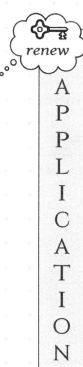

APPLICATION

renew

Date _____ Pray ☐ Annotate ☐ Track ☐ Entry # _____

context
PASSAGE

truths
THEMES

meditate
VERSES

seek
WORDS & PHRASES

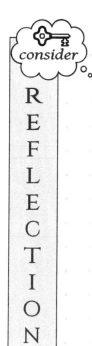

R
E
F
L
E
C
T
I
O
N

consider

A
P
P
L
I
C
A
T
I
O
N

renew

R
E
S
P
O
N
S
E

pray

Date _____ Pray ☐ Annotate ☐ Track ☐ Entry # _____

PASSAGE
context

THEMES
truths

VERSES
meditate

WORDS & PHRASES
seek

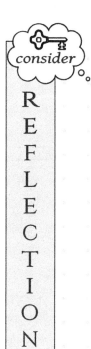

REFLECTION

consider

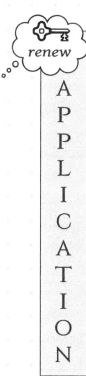

APPLICATION

renew

RESPONSE

pray

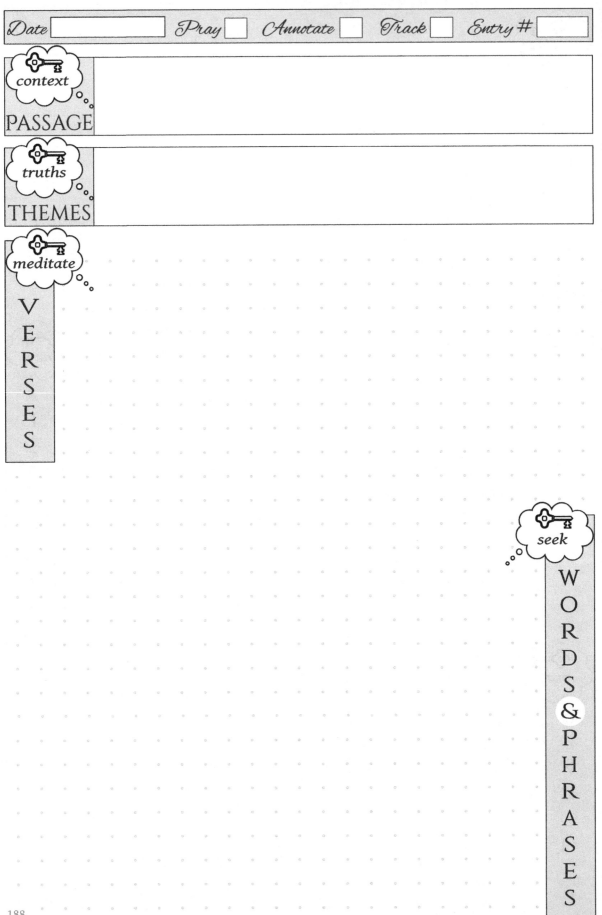

context
PASSAGE

truths
THEMES

meditate
V E R S E S

seek
W O R D S & P H R A S E S

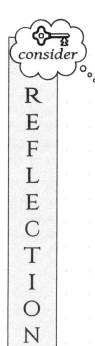

REFLECTION

consider

RESPONSE

pray

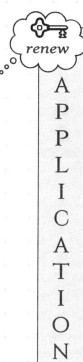

APPLICATION

renew

Date [   ] *Pray* [ ] *Annotate* [ ] *Track* [ ] Entry # [   ]

context
PASSAGE

truths
THEMES

meditate
V
E
R
S
E
S

seek
W
O
R
D
S
&
P
H
R
A
S
E
S

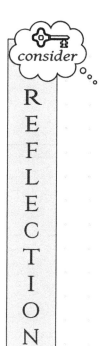

REFLECTION
consider

APPLICATION
renew
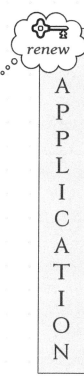

RESPONSE
pray

Date ☐ Pray ☐ Annotate ☐ Track ☐ Entry # ☐

context
PASSAGE

truths
THEMES

meditate
V E R S E S

seek
W O R D S & P H R A S E S

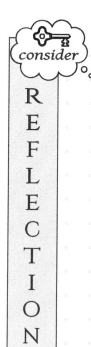

REFLECTION

consider

APPLICATION

renew

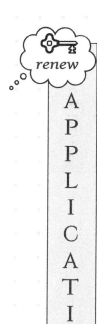

RESPONSE

pray

193

Date | Pray | Annotate | Track | Entry #

context

PASSAGE

truths

THEMES

meditate

VERSES

seek

WORDS & PHRASES

REFLECTION

consider

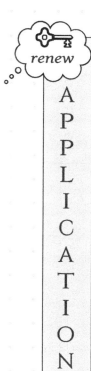

APPLICATION

renew

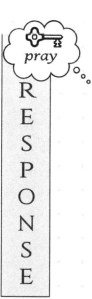

RESPONSE

pray

Date _____ Pray ☐ Annotate ☐ Track ☐ Entry # _____

context
PASSAGE

truths
THEMES

meditate
V E R S E S

seek
W O R D S & P H R A S E S

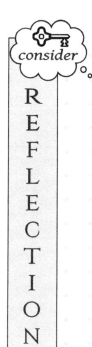

REFLECTION

consider

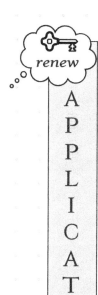

APPLICATION

renew

RESPONSE

pray

context

PASSAGE

truths

THEMES

meditate

V E R S E S

seek

W O R D S & P H R A S E S

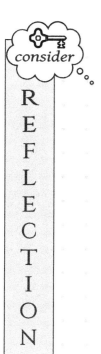

REFLECTION

APPLICATION

RESPONSE